MARGARET ATWOOD

PROCEDURES FOR UNDERGROUND

Toronto
Oxford University Press
1970

Some of these poems were previously published in *The Atlantic Monthly*, *Black Moss*, *Catalyst*, *Duel*, *Edge*, *Ellipse*, *Field*, *Imago*, *Kayak*, *Malahat Review*, *The Merry Devil of Edmonton*, *Prism International*, *Spectrum*, *Stony Brook Poetics*, and *The Tamarack Review*. The author received the Union Poetry Prize from *Poetry* (Chicago) for five poems published in that magazine in 1969: 'Dream: Bluejay or Archeopteryx', 'Three Desk Objects', 'Projected Slide of an Unknown Soldier', 'For Archaeologists', 'Carrying Food Home in Winter' (© 1969 Modern Poetry Association).

Both author and publisher acknowledge assistance from the Canada Council towards completing and publishing this volume.

ISBN — 0-19-540175-1

4 5 6 7 8 - 8 7 6 5 4

Printed in Canada by John Deyell Limited

CONTENTS

CONTENTS

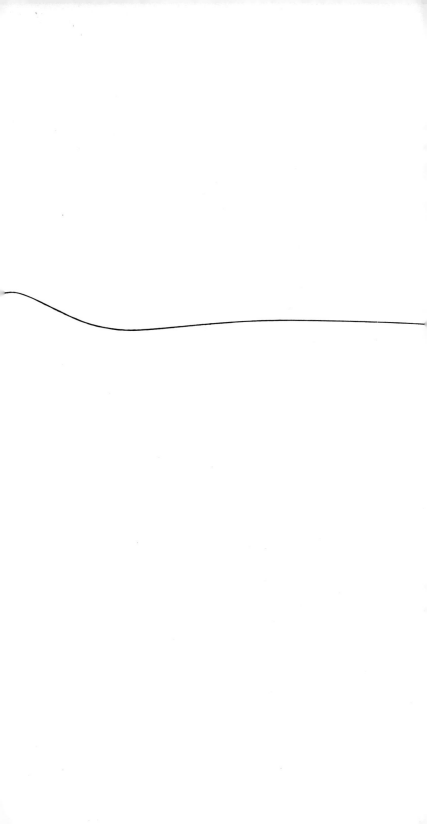

EDEN IS A ZOO

I keep my parents in a garden
among lumpy trees, green sponges
on popsickle sticks. I give them a lopsided
sun which drops its heat
in spokes the colour of yellow crayon.

They have thick elephant legs,
quills for hair and tiny heads;
they clump about under the trees
dressed in the clothes of thirty years
ago, on them innocent as plain skin.

Are they bewildered when they come across
corners of rooms in the forest,
a tin cup shining like pearl,
a frayed pink blanket, a rusted shovel?

Does it bother them to perform
the same actions over and over,
hands gathering white flowers
by the lake or tracing designs in the sand,
a word repeated till it hangs carved
forever in the blue air?

Are they content?

Do they want to get out?

Do they see me looking at them
from across the hedge of spikes
and cardboard fire painted red
I built with so much time
and pain, but
they don't know is there?

GAME AFTER SUPPER

This is before electricity,
it is when there were porches.

On the sagging porch an old man
is rocking. The porch is wooden,

the house is wooden and grey;
in the living room which smells of
smoke and mildew, soon
the woman will light the kerosene lamp.

There is a barn but I am not in the barn;
there is an orchard too, gone bad,
its apples like soft cork
but I am not there either.

I am hiding in the long grass
with my two dead cousins,
the membrane grown already
across their throats.

We hear crickets and our own hearts
close to our ears;
though we giggle, we are afraid.

From the shadows around
the corner of the house
a tall man is coming to find us:

He will be an uncle,
if we are lucky.

DREAM: BLUEJAY
OR ARCHEOPTERYX

kneeling on rock
by lakeside, sun
in the sky and also in
the water, that other
self of mine also
kneeling on rock

on the seared bushes the hard
berries squeezed out from
stem ends in spite of

the red needles crackling
on the ground, the sand, among
the roots, firedry

my four hands gathering
in either world, the berries
in the dish glowed blue
embers

                    a bird
        lit on both branches

    his beak split/ his tin
    scream forked in the air

    warning. above me
    against the sun I saw
    his lizard eye
                    looked
    down.   gone

    in the water
    under my shadow
    there was an outline, man
    surfacing, his body sheathed
    in feathers, his teeth
    glinting like nails, fierce god
    head crested with blue flame

GIRL AND HORSE, 1928

You are younger than I am, you are
someone I never knew, you stand
under a tree, your face half-shadowed,
holding the horse by its bridle.

Why do you smile?   Can't you
see the apple blossoms falling around
you, snow, sun, snow, listen, the tree
dries and is being burnt, the wind

is bending your body, your face
ripples like water   where did you go
But no, you stand there exactly
the same, you can't hear me, forty

years ago you were caught by light
and fixed in that secret
place where we live, where we believe
nothing can change, grow older.

> (On the other side
> of the picture, the instant
> is over, the shadow
> of the tree has moved. You wave,
>
> then turn and ride
> out of sight through the vanished
> orchard, still smiling
> as though you do not notice)

TRANSMIGRATION

The old man with his
scarred heart clamped
between sheets, listening
for the sound of feathers descending
over his head

whose skilled hands once
cut flesh, whipped
horses through mounded
snow, sculpted
muscles, now carves

tiny birds with pins
in their backs. These
he sends to daughters, grand-
daughters   bluejay, kingfisher

hummingbird, its wings outstretched
across my throat, wood
soul

A DIALOGUE

My sister and I share the same
place of recurring dreams

(the lake, the island, the glacier-
smoothed rock, the bay
with low ground, spruce and cedar)

though because we were born in different years
we seldom see each other.

       She says it is a swamp
       at night, she is trying to get away,
       her feet won't move, she is afraid
       of the things that live under the water

       For me it is clear day
       so bright the green pierces,
       but in the distance I hear a motor, a chain-
       saw, the invaders are coming nearer

I passed her at evening, she was running,
her arms stretched out
in front of her; I called but couldn't
wake her

She watched me sinking
among the reeds and lily-pads;
I was smiling, I didn't notice
as the dark lake slipped over my head.

We talk about this in calm voices,
sitting at the kitchen table;
she is examining
her bitten hands, finger
by finger, I draw with a pencil,
covering the page with triangles
and grey geometrical flowers.

THE SMALL CABIN

The house we built gradually
from the ground up when we were young
(three rooms, the walls
raw trees) burned down
last year   they said

I didn't see it, and so
the house is still there in me

among branches as always   I stand
inside it looking out
at the rain moving across the lake

but when I go back
to the empty place in the forest
the house will blaze and crumple
suddenly in my mind

collapsing like a cardboard carton
thrown on a bonfire, summers
crackling, my earlier
selves outlined in flame.

Left in my head will be
the blackened earth: the truth.

Where did the house go?

Where do the words go
when we have said them?

TWO GARDENS

What stands in this garden
is there because I measured, placed, reached
down into the soil and pulled out
stems, leaves, gradually:
                            fabric-
textured zinnias; asters
the colours of chintz; thick
pot-shaped marigolds, the
sunflowers brilliant as
imitations

but outside the string borders

other things raise
themselves, brief
motions at the path's edge

                        the bonewhite
plants that grow
without sunlight, flickering
in the evening forest

certain ferns; fungi
like buried feet
                the blue-
flags, ice flames
reflected in the bay
that melt when the
sun hits noon

these have their roots
in another land

they are mist

if you touch them, your
eyes go through them.

THE SHRUNKEN FOREST

When we were in it we were very small very
small, at least we thought we were small
and it was giant it was too green
for us it was like living
on the surface of the sun (green) only not
burning
            and we were clear
as ice we looked at each
other and saw nothing but a
bending in the air and through
us that element extending placid
as water but it was not water   and now

we are out of it we wonder
whether we were ever there
at all, here light
is so hard and different. Can you doubt
the word of sinks?   of vacuum cleaners?   I would believe
even doorknobs if it were not
for the diagrams of your skull. On one
of them I note, marked
by a dotted line, an area, a bulge
behind your left ear
intensely green and shining
transparent even on this paper,
roughly the size of a thrush's
egg, or a tumour.

DELAYED MESSAGE

As we sat by the shore
one evening, arms around each other
we saw her come out of the lake;

she stood looking at us,
the water up to her ankles;
her hair was black,
she was wearing a grey skirt and a purple sweater.

I know she thought
she was safe on the dry land,
she could feel your hand on her shoulder

(I rose for a long time through
silver, until the light broke
over my head

I saw you there together
against the trees, in the distance the
house door, the lantern

I was wearing a grey
skirt and a purple
sweater, I stood looking at you

through the eyes which were empty holes)

MIDWINTER, PRESOLSTICE

The cold rises around
our house, the wind
drives through the walls in
splinters; on the inside
of the window, behind
the blanket we have hung
a white mould thickens.

We spend the days quietly
trying to be warm; we can't
look through the glass;
in the refrigerator old food
sickens, gives out.

I dream of departures, meetings,
repeated weddings with a stranger, wounded
with knives and bandaged, his
face hidden

        All night my gentle husband
sits alone in the corner
of a grey arena, guarding
a paper bag
        which holds
turnips and apples and my
head, the eyes closed

FRAME

I made this window;
it stands in the middle of my floor.
Around the edges it looks
exactly like a window;

on it I can see
a street, a sidewalk, a blue corner
where birds fly with the jerkiness
of home movies,

the houses where I once lived
cut out of magazines
lined up, one
beside the other;

cardboard figures
of myself, unnaturally short
are propped on each of the lawns
with their backs towards me.

Who left me here?   Who gave me
these scissors?   I dream
always of getting outside.
Nothing opens,
I don't know who to forgive.

34738

WE DON'T LIKE REMINDERS

When they are dry and rattle
in the wind, when their
petals are bloodless, then
we will get rid of them

>   My self compulsively moving
>   objects back from the edges of tables,
>   afraid of falling
>   watching the life drain out of my fingers

Danger danger danger say
the chrysanthemums like
stoplights flashing
once before they go out

>   Yesterday the sun was
>   too quick for me,
>   it got across the sky before
>   I had time to see it.

The cut chrysanthemums sit
on top of my head in a streaked
milk bottle; I hear feet,
someone clipping the grass.

INTERVIEW WITH A TOURIST

You speed by with your camera and your spear
and stop and ask me for directions

I answer there are none

You ask me why the light here
is always the same colour;
I talk about the diffuse
surfaces, angles of refraction

You want to know why there are
no pleasant views, no distances,
why everything crowds close to the skin

I mention the heavier density
here, the thickness, the obsolescence of vistas

You ask me why the men are starved and silver
and have goggle eyes
and why the women are cold tentacled flowers

I reply with a speech about Nature

You ask me why I can't love you

It is because you have air in your lungs
and I am an average citizen

Once, when there was history
some obliterating fact occurred,
no solution was found

Now this country is underwater;
we can love only the drowned

PROCEDURES FOR UNDERGROUND

(Northwest Coast)

The country beneath
the earth has a green sun
and the rivers flow backwards;

the trees and rocks are the same
as they are here, but shifted.
Those who live there are always hungry;

from them you can learn
wisdom and great power,
if you can descend and return safely.

You must look for tunnels, animal
burrows or the cave in the sea
guarded by the stone man;

when you are down you will find
those who were once your friends
but they will be changed and dangerous.

Resist them, be careful
never to eat their food.
Afterwards, if you live, you will be able

to see them when they prowl as winds,
as thin sounds in our village. You will
tell us their names, what they want, who

has made them angry by forgetting them.
For this gift, as for all gifts, you must
suffer: those from the underland

will be always with you, whispering their
complaints, beckoning you
back down; while among us here

you will walk wrapped in an invisible
cloak. Few will seek your help
with love, none without fear.

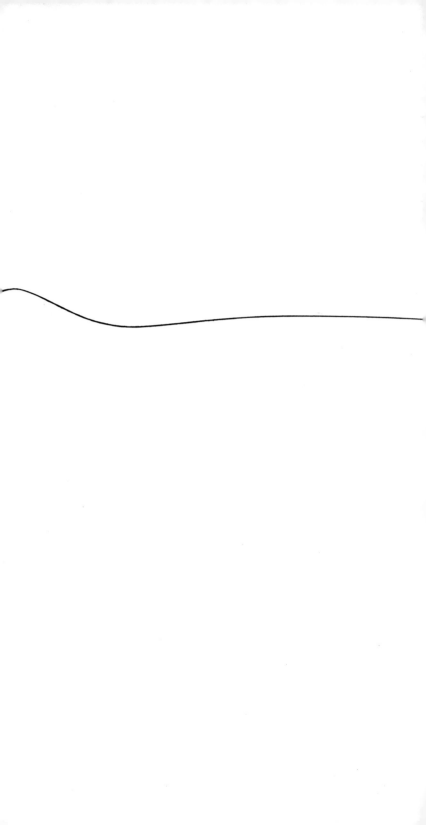

THE CREATURES OF THE ZODIAC

In the daytime I am brave,
I draw my gloves on finger
by finger, my money
behaves itself in my purse
the food rolls over on my plate
there are no omens

I have everything under control

But at night the constellations
emerge; I clench
my feet to boots
my face to a wire mask

Their whitehard eyes bristle
behind the bars, their teeth
grow larger for being starved

They were once dust and ordinary
hatreds. I breathed on them, named them:
now they are predictions.

WEED SEEDS NEAR A BEAVER POND

On the way back to
the pond, following the car track now
only a furrow among saplings

and arms reaching up, in from
the furred sides, hooking hold
of me, rasping, letting go

on the wet bank picked off
from sweater: brown
barbed eggs, arrows, sticky green quills

———————

and objects / barnacles
cups and saucers, plates latch
on to me

when I moved to this city they
moved with me, my skin
is burred with porcelain and gleams

like scales.   like money.   too many
layers of things, too much
time, too heavy

———————

(will they fall off, return to their own
cardboard boxes, loosen
the calendars from me)

there is hope, never keep
a diary, already
there are events I can't remember

and in my brain cells, bone
marrow, parasite molecules, men's faces
unlock, discard

themselves. I chew my fingers, consider
alternatives. I've been used. two
of the dishes broke. replacements. back

there by the pond the winter
day shines down
on air, snow, mud, the waiting

lives I threw away

THE END OF THE WORLD:
WEEKEND, NEAR TORONTO

This is the way it begins:
the countryside almost flat, stretching away
from the four-lane highway, everything
green except for certain
trees which have hardened and stand
grey and fixed in the shapes life gave them,
fossil veins, dead lungs.

The cars are lined up, edging slowly
on the north lanes, the windshields
glitter, it is the city moving,
the drivers intent on getting out, getting
away from something
they carry always with them;
a hand comes out of a window
and throws away an apple core.

The sun shines down

on two cars which have collided
at a turn-off, and rest
quietly on their sides

and on some cows which have come over,
nudge each other aside
at the fence, and stare;
the people in the passing
cars stare too;

out of the blue sky and the white clouds
something is falling   falling
gently on them like invisible rain, or a blessing.

6 A.M., BOSTON, SUMMER SUBLET

Through the screened window
around, above, the leaves and roofs
of August in the gleaming pause
before dust; city
birds making their single note
at the first light, a cricket still
pulsing

down there, the white lawn-
chairs wait round the wooden table;
rain shimmers
in someone else's outdoor grill.

Awake too early, I walk back
and forth across the granular apartment
floorboards: windowsill the border
between this air and a dawn mirage of
water, my mind testing
the outside like a foot

withdrawn. Hidden
things, faint smells
of burning, motors beginning, broken glass.

FOR UNCLE M.

You were affable, sentimental, you liked arguments,
you had to win, you wanted a good time,
you were always frightened.

What were you afraid would happen?
It has happened.

The paisley dressing gown
hangs in the closet, diminished, the gold
cufflinks that became
solid by clinging to your wrists   fade/
you shadow the threshold, a smell
of shaving lotion, frightened,
hovering at the edges of heavy
objects, wanting me to admit
you are real. Were real.   How can I

In this cubicle
above the city, among your rubbery
potted plants and china statues
and your reflection jittering on the T.V.
I can give you only a fresh evasion;

How can I pretend you were happy?

(But now I think: each spring
you went to a small house on swamp-
land by the river. I never saw it

I will admit the beets
were real.
                I go around to the back:
see, I have come, I can't stay long,
I promise to talk finally
while we have time, I stretch out my hand

The man on his knees
among the onions and feathery carrot
tops keeps his back to me, his head
is bent; he is weeding the vegetables.
The sky is clear, there is no sound
but the dry cicadas and
the faint scrape of his trowel.

HYPOTHESES: CITY

To get out of this fear enclosing
me like rubber, like a diving
suit, the breath
measured and strapped on my shoulders

to get rid of the spear

and swim the city freely, among
its people, the streets, rooms,
as though it were entirely natural

But even fish have territories
and go armed

What then
            to be

the water
itself, the water all
float in and none notice, to
be everywhere and nothing

as I was now

(they walk
through me, not seeing
me)

> my eyes diffused, washing
> in waves of light across the ceiling,

> my neck on the back of this chair.

STORIES IN KINSMAN'S PARK

We take the children to the park
where there are swings,
a wading pool;

their father is in the hospital,
the latest scar contracting
across his scalp.

When they are tired of water
and climbing, we tell stories,
making witches from coloured wool.

> In the sun all wounds
> are imaginary or cured
> by secret leaves, the green place
> expands around us, holds us
> enclosed, the high
> voices of children immerse
> us, quick and continuous as insects
>
> Here, we are convinced
> death can occur only
> to witches and in
> the sanctioned ways. The victorious
> children live, as they should,
> in the forest forever.

Cars start; the day re-enters
us, the pool water is gone
before we notice.

Driving for home,
the older one wants to know
how to stop thunder;
he says he is afraid of things
that get in through the windows.

The younger says
he is afraid of nothing;
he is the one who wants

the light on, who has
bad dreams, the caterpillar
eating the side of his head.

DREAMS OF THE ANIMALS

Mostly the animals dream
of other animals   each
according to its kind

> (though certain mice and small rodents
> have nightmares of a huge pink
> shape with five claws descending)

: moles dream of darkness and delicate
mole smells

frogs dream of green and golden
frogs
sparkling like wet suns
among the lilies

red and black
striped fish, their eyes open
have red and black striped
dreams   defence, attack, meaningful
patterns

birds dream of territories
enclosed by singing.

Sometimes the animals dream of evil
in the form of soap and metal
but mostly the animals dream
of other animals.

There are exceptions:

the silver fox in the roadside zoo
dreams of digging out
and of baby foxes, their necks bitten

the caged armadillo
near the train
station, which runs
all day in figure eights
its piglet feet pattering,
no longer dreams
but is insane when waking;

the iguana
in the petshop window on St Catherine Street
crested, royal-eyed, ruling
its kingdom of water-dish and sawdust

dreams of sawdust.

CYCLOPS

You, going along the path,
mosquito-doped, with no moon, the flashlight
a single orange eye

unable to see what is beyond
the capsule of your dim
sight, what shape

contracts to a heart
with terror, bumps
among the leaves, what makes
a bristling noise like a fur throat

Is it true you do not wish to hurt them?

Is it true you have no fear?
Take off your shoes then,

let your eyes go bare,
swim in their darkness as in a river

do not disguise
yourself in armour.

They watch you from hiding:
you are a chemical
smell, a cold fire, you are
giant and indefinable

In their monstrous night
thick with possible claws
where danger is not knowing,

you are the hugest monster.

THREE DESK OBJECTS

What suns had to rise and set
what eyes had to blink out
what hands and fingers
had to let go of their heat

before you appeared on my desk
black light
portable and radiant

and you, my electric typewriter
with your cord and hungry plug
drinking a sinister transfusion
from the other side of the wall

what histories of slaughter
have left these scars on your keys

What multiple deaths have set loose this clock
the small wheels that grind
their teeth under the metal scalp

My cool machines
resting there so familiar
so hard and perfect

I am afraid to touch you
I think you will cry out in pain

I think you will be warm, like skin.

SPELL FOR THE DIRECTOR OF PROTOCOL

You would like to keep me
from saying anything: you would prefer it
if when I opened my mouth
nothing came out
but a white comic-strip balloon
with a question mark; or a blank button.

Sometimes you put it more strongly,
I can feel your thumbs
on my windpipe, you would like me to stutter,
I can feel you nailing STOP signs
all over my skin on the inside;
you would like me to sign my name, finally.

I remember when I first knew
you were there, it was when I was running,
perhaps I inhaled you.
But there is one word among all the others,
if I could say it in time
the badges tacked to my heart would melt:

a word like an unclenching flower.
It will use all my breath,
my lungs will be squeezed dry;
but at least it will get you out
into the red light, the falling cinders
where I can see you.

PROJECTED SLIDE
OF AN UNKNOWN SOLDIER

Upon the wall a face
uttered itself
in light, pushing
aside the wall's darkness;

Around it leaves, glossy,
perhaps tropical, not making
explicit whether the face was
breaking through them, wore them
as disguise, was crowned
with them or sent them
forth as rays,
a slippery halo;

The clothes were invisible,
the eyes
hidden; the nose
foreshortened: a muzzle.
Hair on the upper lip.
On the skin the light shone, wet
with heat; the teeth
of the open mouth reflected it
as absolute.

The mouth was open
stretched wide in a call or howl
(there was no tongue)
of agony, ultimate
command or simple famine.
The canine teeth ranged back
into the throat and vanished.

The mouth was filled with darkness.
The darkness in the open mouth
uttered itself, pushing
aside the light.

COMIC BOOKS VS. HISTORY
(1949, 1969)

On the blackboard map your country
was erased, blank, waiting
to be filled with whatever shapes
we chose:

               tense
needle turrets of steel
cities
               heroes
lived there, we knew

they all wore capes, bullets
bounced off them;
from their fists came beautiful
orange collisions.

Our side was coloured in
with dots and letters

but it held only
real-sized explorers, confined
to animal skin coats;

they plodded, discovered
rivers whose names we always
forgot; in the winters
they died of scurvy.

When I reached that other
shore finally, statistics
and diseased labels multiplied
everywhere in my head

space contracted, the
red and silver
heroes had collapsed inside
their rubber suits / the riddled
buildings were decaying
magic

I turn back, search
for the actual, collect lost
bones, burnt logs
of campfires, pieces of fur.

RETURN TRIPS WEST

1

We follow the cement paths
conscientious with flower borders;
you name the buildings, one after another.

The walls turn towards me
smooth, uninformative;

for you they are bunched with menace,
their bricks ripple and bulge.

In front of you everywhere goes another man,
scowling at you from doorways,

ignoring you in the cafeteria
with its wooden plaques and antlers,

as we cross the bridge glancing
with scorn back over his shoulder,
his eyes phosphorescent.

2

This is a place I can't enter
and neither can you, finally.

What you thought
you would find here has

vanished, as if
the moment you left, the town
heaved like a wave,

the houses tip on their
foundations, the roofs are collapsing, the
wires thrash,

in the wash of new neon
light, the shadowy faces
including your own, float
silently, go under

3

Later as you sleep
in the car, I watch your face
alter, I know

you have gone back to the town / the only
way you can ever get there;

you run over the bridge, you begin
to climb the mountain, you reach
the rocks, the forgotten absence, the

desolation. I am not with you, I will
never be with you; even

in daytime I can
only ask questions
which define my failure.

What can be shared?

84th STREET, EDMONTON

So this is it, flat
edmonton, me walking back
from the store carrying
two gallons of white paint
and pausing at the corners
to rest in this silence where the streets
have no names but only numbers:

pink stucco houses, paleblue
horizon too near, enamel
cars in rows, highrises, trees
with red berries, that's
something at any rate
though it will hardly get me through the winter.

The pain in my fingers is
the only thing that's real, the houses,
trees, parked cars are
a tight surface covering
panic or only more
nothing than I've ever seen

I could stop. This could be where
I stop finally. I could
disappear, say
at the next driveway; but

courage, genesis descends
here also or never

I will build a history
in the backyard from solid
rocks, populate it
with dried sticks and the old newspaper-
faced gods

covered by twilight and the first
white snow.

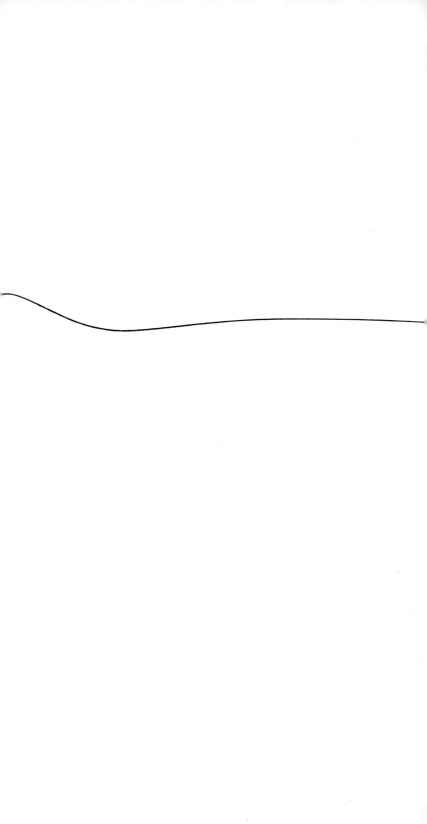

HIGHEST ALTITUDE

Here, our possessions are cut
to what we carry: plates,

blanket, our maps, basket with food,
last thought: lake where we waded
in the green glacial water.

The view to the side, below,
would be, as they say, breath-

taking; if we dared to look.
We don't dare. The curved

ledge is crumbling, the melting snow
is undermining the road,

in fear everything
lives, impermanence
makes the edges of things burn

brighter. The rocks are purple, heart-
red. We hold our eyes tight
to the line; the reference point

not the mountains but the moving
car, and each other.

A MORNING

Because we couldn't sleep we went on
though at first I could see little;

behind us the sun rose
white and cold; the early
wind came out of the sun.

In front of us the low hills, yellow-
grey grass dunes, and then
the mountains: hard, furrowed
with erosion, cloudless, old, new,
abrupt in the first light.

With shrunken fingers
we ate our oranges and bread,
shivering in the parked car;

though we knew we had never
been there before,
we knew we had been there before.

A SOUL, GEOLOGICALLY

The longer we stay here the harder
it is for me to see you.

Your outline, skin
that marks you off
melts in this light

and from behind your face
the unknown areas appear:

hills yellow-pelted, dried earth
bubbles, or thrust up
steeply as knees

the sky a flat blue desert,

these spaces you fill
with their own emptiness.

Your shape wavers, glares
like heat above the road,

then you merge and extend:
you have gone,
in front of me there is a stone ridge.

Which of these forms
have you taken:

hill, tree clawed
to the rock, fallen rocks worn
and rounded by the wind

You are the wind,
you contain me

I walk in the white silences
of your mind, remembering

the way it is millions of years before
on the wide floor of the sea

while my eyes lift like continents
to the sun and erode slowly.

HABITATION

Marriage is not
a house or even a tent

it is before that, and colder:

the edge of the forest, the edge
of the desert
            the unpainted stairs
at the back where we squat
outside, eating popcorn

the edge of the receding glacier

where painfully and with wonder
at having survived even
this far

we are learning to make fire

CHRYSANTHEMUMS:
                              a gift:
orange flowers in a water blue
green room

given to the eyes
as the oval stones
we found on the shore
were not found but given
to the hands

as the light each morning.

By themselves in the cupboard
where I put them, the stones grow
luminous within; for their own
reasons the flowers
in the dark send out
their scent: invisible petals

We think of them and know
we possess nothing

but still there are the gifts

(we borrow
time from each other)

and colours, forms, the present
flowers must be
to us in these last days
(each hour we enter
the room, silent
orange explosion)

as brilliant images the eyes
are said to see
the instant before drowning.

TWO VERSIONS OF SWEATERS

1

The washed sweaters, your
cast skins drying on the floor
hold you still in
outline

Decapitated, legless, their
bodies flattened, they stretch out
their arms taut
with agony, calling
silently into the newspaper space

2

Two sweaters have been added:
smaller, white and orange

new phases of me which are
orange, white.

These temporary
forms do not lie
in rows neatly

but soar, diagonal, upside-
down, their colours
tense as wings
with joy of flight or

(tatters anyway
after a few years, burnt
by the flesh they cover / the live
bones are embers)

bright ashes, blown
upwards from a shapeless fire

WOMAN SKATING

A lake sunken among
cedar and black spruce hills;
late afternoon.

On the ice a woman skating,
jacket sudden
red against the white,

concentrating on moving
in perfect circles.

> (actually she is my mother, she is
> over at the outdoor skating rink
> near the cemetery. On three sides
> of her there are streets of brown
> brick houses; cars go by; on the
> fourth side is the park building.
> The snow banked around the rink
> is grey with soot. She never skates
> here. She's wearing a sweater and
> faded maroon earmuffs, she has
> taken off her gloves)

Now near the horizon
the enlarged pink sun swings down.
Soon it will be zero.

With arms wide the skater
turns, leaving her breath like a diver's
trail of bubbles.

Seeing the ice
as what it is, water:
seeing the months
as they are, the years
in sequence occurring
underfoot, watching
the miniature human
figure balanced on steel
needles (those compasses
floated in saucers) on time
sustained, above
time circling: miracle

Over all I place
a glass bell

YOUNGER SISTER, GOING SWIMMING

(Northern Quebec)

Beside this lake
where there are no other people

my sister in bathing suit continues
her short desolate
parade to the end of the dock;

against the boards
her feet make sad statements
she thinks no one can hear;

(I sit in a deckchair
not counting, invisible;
the sun wavers on
this page as on a pool.)

She moves the raft out
past the sandy point;
no one comes by in a motorboat.

She would like to fill the lake
with other swimmers, with answers.
She calls her name. The sun encloses
rocks, trees, her feet in the water, the circling
bays and hills as before.

She poises, raises her arms
as though signalling, then disappears.
The lake heals itself quietly
of the wound left by the diver.
The air quakes and is still.

(Under my hand the paper
closes over these
marks I am making on it.

The words ripple, subside,
move outwards toward the shore.)

FISHING FOR EEL TOTEMS

I stood on the reed bank
ear tuned to the line, listening
to the signals from the ones who lived
under the blue barrier,

thinking they had no words for things
in the air.

The string jumped,
I hooked a martian / it poured
fluid silver out of the river

its long body whipped on the grass, reciting
all the letters of its alphabet.

Killed, it was a
grey tongue hanged silent in the smokehouse

which we later ate.

After that I could see
for a time in the green country;

I learned that the earliest language
was not our syntax of chained pebbles

but liquid, made
by the first tribes, the fish
people.

BUFFALO IN COMPOUND: ALBERTA

The marsh flat where they graze
beside the stream is
late afternoon, serene
with slanted light: green leaves are
yellow: even
the mud shines

Placid, they bend down
silently to the grass;
when they move, the small birds
follow, settle almost
under their feet.

Fenced out but anxious
anyway, and glad our car is
near, we press
close to the wire
squares, our hands raised
for shields
against the sun, which is
everywhere

It was hard to see them
but we thought we saw
in the field near them, the god
of this place: brutal,
zeus-faced, his horned
head man-bearded, his
fused red eye turned inward
to cloudburst and pounded earth, the water-
falling of hooves fisted inside
a calm we would call madness.

Then they were going
in profile, one by one, their
firelit outlines fixed as carvings

backs to us now
they enter
the shade of the gold-edged trees

FOR ARCHEOLOGISTS

Deep under, far back
the early horses run
on rock   /   the buffalo, the deer
the other animals (extinct)
run with spears in their backs

Made with blood, with coloured
dirt, with smoke, not meant
to be seen but to remain
there hidden, potent
in the dark, the link between
the buried will and the upper
world of sun and green feeding,
chase and the hungry kill

drawn by a hand hard
even to imagine

but passed on
in us, part of us now
part of the structure of the bones

existing still in us
as fossil skulls
of the bear, spearheads, bowls and
folded skeletons arranged
in ritual patterns, waiting
for the patient searcher to find them

exist in caves of the earth.

CARRYING FOOD HOME IN WINTER

I walk uphill through the snow
hard going
brown paper bag of groceries
balanced low on my stomach,
heavy, my arms stretching
to hold it turn all tendon.

Do we need this paper bag
my love, do we need this bulk
of peels and cores, do we need
these bottles, these roots
and bits of cardboard
to keep us floating
as on a raft
above the snow I sink through?

The skin creates
islands of warmth
in winter, in summer
islands of coolness.

The mouth performs
a similar deception.

I say I will transform
this egg into a muscle
this bottle into an act of love

This onion will become a motion
this grapefruit
will become a thought.

FRAGMENTS: BEACH

1

At first we know
we intrude, like thrown
bottles, junk metal

but the place grinds us

piece of glass we
found, turned by the
stones into a stone

2

We arrange the beach, build
a driftwood hut out of the empty
huts; the fallen
walls teach us
how to build
                    we pack
barricades of sand

which blows into
blankets, shoes, our tight
containers
                the beach
                arranges us

3

the tent a
skin stretched over
our eyes is a new
sense
      lets in
grass noises rasping, weed-
taste of mist, shiver
of early moon, a different
light

4

In the afternoon the sun
expands, we enter
its hot perimeter
               our feet
burn, our hair lifts
incandescent, the waves
are chill fire, clean
us to bone

5

the surf scours our ears

wind bends
the sand around us

the shapes we make
in the sand from lying down
are salt, are brown, are
flesh

6

light is a sound
            it roars
it fills us
        we swell with it
are strenuous, vast

rocks

hurl our voices / we

are abolished

7

In the night the tents
the driftwood
walls, the sleepers

lose their hold
on shore, are drawn
out on a gigantic tide

we also make the slow deep
circle
        until
the sea returns us

leaves us
absolved, washed
shells on the morning beach

DANCING PRACTICE

1

My parents and some others.
practise their country dances
feet thumping on the living-
room floor
to music from the record player.

Awkward hops/ knees crack/ the plump
woman skids, gets mixed up,
the redfaced man counts
under his breath;
on the mantlepiece the flowered tea-
cups jiggle.

Myself and friends watching
near the wall, clap our hands and smile,
feeling superior and younger.

2

In a minute the record
will be over, they will stop, we
will applaud politely, they will take their coats,
say good-bye, they will be gone;
we will sit and talk, the clock hands
whipping round, the dance
whose pattern we could not
see almost forgotten;
then it will be night,
then morning; we
will sleep, yawn, ponderously
get up
        The dancers
will recede from us, be lost
among the thousands of things that once happened.

3

But the dance itself, the way
it should have been, goes
on in a different
time   (because
        I say it)

where precise as
crystals the new feet
of the dancers move
across a green lawn at evening

the music now
sounding from everywhere

or is it a beach, the sun rising

their faces turning, their changed hands
meeting and letting go, the circle
forming, breaking, each
one of them the whole
rhythm (snow on the tree
branches)
            transformed
            for this moment/   always

(because I say)

the sea   the shore